T0120373

TIGER SHARK VS. LEOPARD SEAL

BY NATHAN SOMMER

BELLWETHER MEDIA • MINNEAPOLIS, MN

Torque brims with excitement perfect for thrill-seekers of all kinds. Discover daring survival skills, explore uncharted worlds, and marvel at mighty engines and extreme sports. In *Torque* books, anything can happen. Are you ready?

This edition first published in 2023 by Bellwether Media, Inc.

No part of this publication may be reproduced in whole or in part without written permission of the publisher. For information regarding permission, write to Bellwether Media, Inc., Attention: Permissions Department, 6012 Blue Circle Drive, Minnetonka, MN 55343.

Library of Congress Cataloging-in-Publication Data

Names: Sommer, Nathan, author.
Title: Tiger shark vs. leopard seal / by Nathan Sommer.
Other titles: Tiger shark versus leopard seal
Description: Minneapolis, MN : Bellwether Media, Inc., 2023. | Series: Torque. Animal battles. | Includes bibliographical references and index. | Audience: Ages 7-12 | Audience: Grades 4-6 | Summary: "Amazing photography accompanies engaging information about the fighting advantages of tiger sharks and leopard seals. The combination of high-interest subject matter and light text is intended for students in grades 3 through 7"– Provided by publisher.
Identifiers: LCCN 2022038239 (print) | LCCN 2022038240 (ebook) | ISBN 9798886871678 (library binding) | ISBN 9798886872156 (paperback) | ISBN 9798886872934 (ebook)
Subjects: LCSH: Tiger shark–Juvenile literature. | Leopard seal–Juvenile literature.
Classification: LCC QL638.95.C3 S66 2023 (print) | LCC QL638.95.C3 (ebook) | DDC 597.3/4–dc23/eng/20220829
LC record available at https://lccn.loc.gov/2022038239
LC ebook record available at https://lccn.loc.gov/2022038240

Editor: Kieran Downs   Designer: Josh Brink

Printed in the United States of America, North Mankato, MN.

TABLE OF CONTENTS

THE COMPETITORS

Tiger sharks are some of the ocean's deadliest **predators**. These beasts hunt whatever they can find, including other tiger sharks! Most **prey** cannot escape them.

But tiger sharks are not the only predators in the water. Leopard seals are fast and **aggressive** in water and on land. What happens when these two predators battle?

Tiger sharks are named for the tigerlike stripes across their backs. They have broad heads, long fins, and large upper tails. Some grow up to 25 feet (7.6 meters) long and weigh up to 1,900 pounds (862 kilograms).

Tiger sharks are found in warm oceans worldwide. They prefer open coasts and busy **coral reefs**.

GARBAGE EATERS

Tiger sharks may accidentally eat garbage. Old tires and license plates have been found in their stomachs.

TIGER SHARK PROFILE

|---|---|---|---|---|---|
| 0 | 5 FEET | 10 FEET | 15 FEET | 20 FEET | 25 FEET |

LENGTH
UP TO 25 FEET
(7.6 METERS)

WEIGHT
UP TO 1,900 POUNDS
(862 KILOGRAMS)

HABITAT

WARM OCEANS

CORAL REEFS

TIGER SHARK RANGE

■ RANGE

LEOPARD SEAL PROFILE

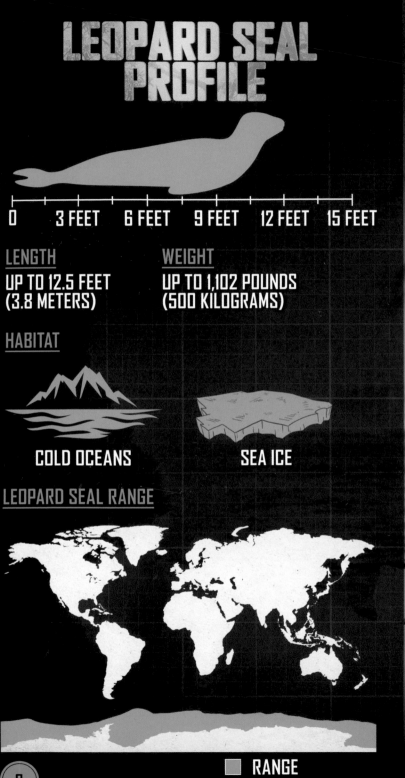

0   3 FEET   6 FEET   9 FEET   12 FEET   15 FEET

LENGTH
UP TO 12.5 FEET
(3.8 METERS)

WEIGHT
UP TO 1,102 POUNDS
(500 KILOGRAMS)

HABITAT

COLD OCEANS   SEA ICE

LEOPARD SEAL RANGE

RANGE

Leopard seals are named after their spotted coats. They have slim bodies, long heads, and large flippers. The largest are 12.5 feet (3.8 meters) long and weigh up to 1,102 pounds (500 kilograms).

Leopard seals are the only seals to regularly eat warm-blooded prey. Most live in cold waters near Antarctica.

SECRET WEAPONS

Tiger sharks use **camouflage** to hunt. Their blueish-gray backs are hard to see from above. Yellowish-white bellies make them hard to spot from below.

Large flippers help leopard seals reach speeds of up to 25 miles (40.2 kilometers) per hour. This allows them to chase down most prey. Their flippers also help them climb onto land to escape enemies.

SECRET WEAPONS

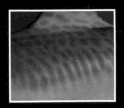

CAMOUFLAGE

STRONG SENSES

SERRATED TEETH

Tiger sharks have strong senses. Their **snouts** feel the movements of prey swimming nearby. The sharks can also smell blood in the water up to 1,320 feet (402 meters) away.

LEOPARD SEAL

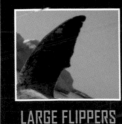  

| LARGE FLIPPERS | POWERFUL JAWS | SHARP TEETH |

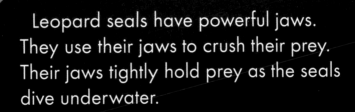

Leopard seals have powerful jaws. They use their jaws to crush their prey. Their jaws tightly hold prey as the seals dive underwater.

Tiger sharks have pointed, **serrated** teeth. They grow up to 2 inches (5 centimeters) long. These easily slice into prey. Their teeth are sharp enough to cut through a turtle's shell!

REPLACEABLE TEETH

If tiger sharks lose a tooth, another one always grows back!

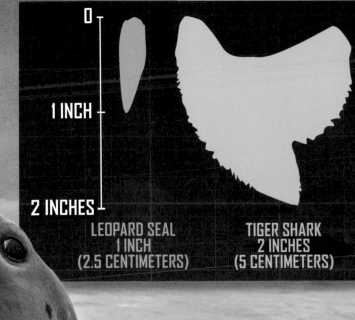

0

1 INCH

2 INCHES

LEOPARD SEAL
1 INCH
(2.5 CENTIMETERS)

TIGER SHARK
2 INCHES
(5 CENTIMETERS)

Leopard seals also have sharp teeth. Their **canine teeth** grow up to 1 inch (2.5 centimeters) long. They use these to bite enemies and tear into prey.

15

ATTACK MOVES

Tiger sharks are aggressive hunters. They eat whatever they can capture. The predators **stalk** their prey. They swim up slowly and attack at the right moment.

Leopard seals are **opportunistic** hunters. They hunt whatever they can find. The seals wait underwater near **ice shelves**. They grab prey the second it enters the water!

WATER AND LAND

Leopard seals mostly hunt in water. They go on land to rest and raise their young.

Tiger sharks use long tails to charge forward in a quick attack! They ram into prey to stun it. Small prey is swallowed whole. Large food is torn into smaller pieces.

Leopard seals slam prey against the water once they catch it. This tears the prey into smaller pieces. The small pieces are easy for the seals to eat.

PREY FOR ORCAS

Orcas are the only major predator to both tiger sharks and leopard seals.

READY, FIGHT!

A leopard seal slides into the water. It is quickly met by a hungry tiger shark. The shark charges at the seal. It gives the seal a big bite!

The seal bites the shark back. Its sharp teeth surprise the shark. The seal quickly pulls itself back onto land. Its speed helped it get away from the tiger shark!

GLOSSARY

aggressive—ready to fight

camouflage—colors and patterns that help an animal hide in its surroundings

canine teeth—long, pointed teeth that are often the sharpest in the mouth

coral reefs—structures made of coral that usually grow in shallow seawater

ice shelves—large floating platforms of ice

opportunistic—taking advantage of a situation

predators—animals that hunt other animals for food

prey—animals that are hunted by other animals for food

serrated—having a blade like that of a saw

snouts—the nose and mouth areas on some animals

stalk—to follow closely and quietly

TO LEARN MORE

AT THE LIBRARY

Adamson, Thomas K. *Great White Shark vs. Killer Whale.*
Minneapolis, Minn.: Bellwether Media, 2020.

Jaycox, Jaclyn. *This or That Questions About Antarctica: You Decide!* North Mankato, Minn.: Capstone Press, 2022.

Rose, Rachel. *Tiger Shark.* Minneapolis, Minn.: Bearport Publishing Company, 2022.

ON THE WEB

FACTSURFER

Factsurfer.com gives you a safe, fun way to find more information.

1. Go to www.factsurfer.com

2. Enter "tiger shark vs. leopard seal" into the search box and click 🔍

3. Select your book cover to see a list of related content.

INDEX

The images in this book are reproduced through the courtesy of: Tomas Kotouc, cover (tiger shark), p. 2 (serrated teeth); Tarpan, cover, (leopard seal), p. 13 (powerful jaws); Amanda Cotton/ Alamy Stock Photo, pp. 2-3, 20-21, 22-23, 24 (shark); Steve Jones/ Stocktrek Images/ Alamy Stock Photo, pp. 2-3, 20-21, 22-23, 24 (seal); Matt9122, pp. 4, 12 (strong senses); WorldFoto/ Alamy Stock Photo, p. 5; Miguel Lasa/ Steve Bloom Images/ Alamy Stock Photo, pp. 6-7; antony baxter/ Alamy Stock Photo, pp. 8-9; Cultura Creative RF/ Alamy Stock Photo, p. 10; Steve Jones/ Alamy Stock Photo, p. 11; HQuality, p. 12 (camouflage); Howard Chew/ Alamy Stock Photo, p. 12 (tiger shark); Antcold, p. 13 (large flippers); Jan Matin Will, p. 13 (sharp teeth); Alf Jacob Nilsen/ Alamy Stock Photo, p. 13 (seal); Todd Mintz/ Alamy Stock Photo, p. 14; Danita Delimont/ Alamy Stock Photo, p. 15; Andrey Nekrasov/ Alamy Stock Photo, p. 16; Paul Souders/ Getty Images, p. 17; Auscape/ Getty Images, p. 18; JoeFox Liverpool/ Alamy Stock Photo, p. 19.